WALK AROUND

F-16 FIGHTING FALCON

By Lou Drendel

Walk Around Number 1

squadron/signal publications

Introduction

Our several walks around various F-16s for the photographs in this book were nearly a coast-to-coast operation. We started with F-16Cs and F-16Ds of the Fighter Weapons Center at Nellis AFB, Nevada. We visited the F-16A and F-16Bs of the Illinois Air National Guard at Springfield, IL. and an F-16D of the 17th Fighter Squadron, Hooters, of the 363rd Fighter Wing. It was a quick but through tour which gave us ample opportunity to shoot a great variety of detail.

The F-16 Fighting Falcon (a.k.a. Viper and Electric Jet) has become the F-4 Phantom of the '90s. As this is written, over 3,000 F-16s have been delivered with another 800 plus on order. The F-16 is flown by eighteen different countries. It has proven itself to be an outstanding performer in combat and is likely to be around well into the next century.

Although it started as a simple, clear-air air superiority fighter, designed by the so-called "Fighter Mafia" to be a light weight fighter. The F-16 has evolved into an all-weather fighter- bomber. It is a classic fighter ... single pilot, single engine. But it is far from simple. State-of-the-art avionics and computer software enable the F-16 to carry most of the air-to-air and air-to-ground munitions in the Unites States' arsenal. Since much of the evolution of the F-16 has taken place in it's computer software, the basic shape of the Viper remains much the same as that of the first LWF prototype

This FSD F-16A had the original small horizontal tail surfaces and was also equipped with flight test cameras where the chaff/flare dispensers are normally located. The aircraft also carried an instrumented nose probe.

COPYRIGHT © 1993 SQUADRON/SIGNAL PUBLICATIONS, INC.
1115 CROWLEY DRIVE   CARROLLTON, TEXAS 75011-5010

ISBN 0-89747-307-8

If you have any photographs of the aircraft, armor, soldiers or ships of any nation, particularly wartime snapshots, why not share them with us and help make Squadron/Signal's books all the more interesting and complete in the future. Any photograph sent to us will be copied and the original returned. The donor will be fully credited for any photos used. Please send them to:

Squadron/Signal Publications, Inc.
1115 Crowley Drive.
Carrollton, TX 75011-5010.

Acknowledgements

USAF
General Dynamics
G.L. Davis/Focal Plane Imagery
C.A. Neill/Focal Plane Imagery
Ted Carlson

David F. Brown
Glenn Ashley
Norm Taylor
Chris Reed
Roy Chismar

Exterior Inspection

NOTE: Check aircraft condition for loose doors & fasteners, cracks, dents, leaks and other discrepancies.

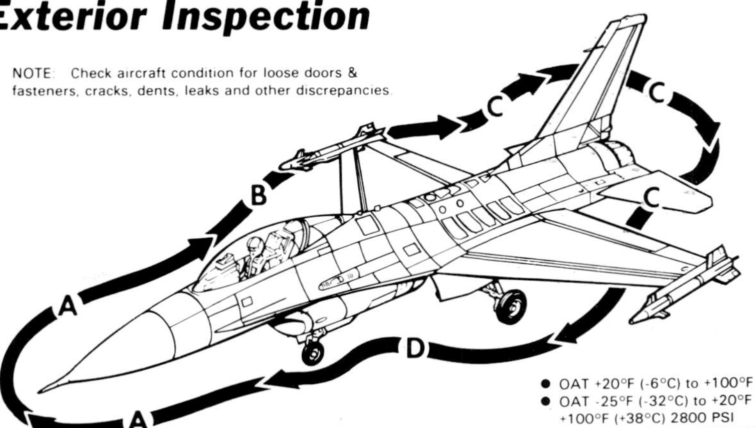

- OAT +20°F (-6°C) to +100°F (+38°C) 3000 PSI
- OAT -25°F (-32°C) to +20°F (-6°C) or above +100°F (+38°C) 2800 PSI
- OAT below -25°F (-32°C) 3200 PSI

NOSE

A 1. FORWARD FUSELAGE:
   - A. CANOPY EXTERNAL JETTISON HANDLES (2) — SECURE.
   - B. PITOT STATIC PROBES (2) — CONDITION.
   - C. AOA PROBES (2) — CONDITION.
   - D. STATIC PORTS (2) — CONDITION
   - E. DE [NO] IDENTIFICATION LIGHT — CONDITION.
   - F. RADOME — SECURE.
   - G. ENGINE INLET DUCT — CLEAR.
   - H. [5] EPU FIRED INDICATOR — CHECK.
   - I. ECS RAM INLET DUCTS — CLEAR.

CENTER FUSELAGE & RIGHT WING

B 1. RIGHT MLG:
   - A. TIRE, WHEEL AND STRUT — CONDITION.
   - B. UPLOCK ROLLER — CHECK.
   - C. DOOR LINKAGE — SECURE.
   - D. LG SAFETY PIN — INSTALLED.
   - E. TAXI LIGHT — CONDITION.
2. RIGHT WING:
   - A. HYDRAZINE DETECTOR — CHECK.
   - B. EPU NITROGEN BOTTLE — CHARGED.
   - C. HYDRAULIC SYSTEM A QUANTITY AND ACCUMULATOR — CHECK.
   - D. GUN RNDS COUNTER AND RNDS LIMIT — SET.
   - E. SECURE VOICE PROCESSOR — CHECK.
   - F. EPU EXHAUST PORT — CONDITION.
   - G. LEF — CONDITION.
   - H. EXTERNAL STORES AND PYLONS — SECURE.
   - I. NAVIGATION & FORMATION LIGHTS — CONDITION.
   - J. FLAPERON — CONDITION.

AFT FUSELAGE

C 1. TAIL:
   - A. ENGINE ACCESSORY DRIVE GEARBOX — CHECK.
   - B. BRAKE JFS ACCUMULATORS — CHARGED.
   - C. ARRESTING HOOK — CONDITION AND PIN FREE TO MOVE.
   - D. [NO] DRAG CHUTE ACCUMULATOR — CHARGED.
   - E. VENTRAL FINS, SPEEDBRAKES, HORIZONTAL TAILS, RUDDER — CONDITION.
   - F. [NO] DRAG CHUTE HOUSING — CONDITION.
   - G. ENGINE EXHAUST AREA — CONDITION.
   - H. NAVIGATION AND FORMATION LIGHTS — CONDITION.
   - I. [39] VERTICAL TAIL LIGHT — CONDITION.
   - J. FLCS ACCUMULATORS — CHARGED.
   - K. JFS DOORS/LOUVERS — CLOSED.

LEFT WING & CENTER FUSELAGE

D 1. LEFT WING:
   - A. FLAPERON — CONDITION.
   - B. NAVIGATION & FORMATION LIGHTS — CONDITION.
   - C. EXTERNAL STORES AND PYLONS — SECURE.
   - D. LEF — CONDITION.
   - E. FUEL VENT OUTLET — CLEAR.
   - F. HYDRAULIC SYSTEM B QUANTITY AND ACCUMULATOR — CHECK.
2. LEFT MLG:
   - A. TIRE, WHEEL AND STRUT — CONDITION.
   - B. UPLOCK ROLLER — CHECK.
   - C. DOORS AND LINKAGE — SECURE.
   - D. LG SAFETY PIN — INSTALLED.
   - E. LG PIN POUCH — CHECK CONDITION.
   - F. LANDING LIGHT — CONDITION.
3. FUSELAGE:
   - A. GUN PORT — CONDITION.
   - B. IFF MODE 4 — CHECK.
   - C. AVTR — CHECK.
4. UNDERSIDE:
   - A. NLG TIRE, WHEEL AND STRUT — CONDITION.
   - B. NLG SCISSORS LINK PIN AND LG SAFETY PIN — INSTALLED.
   - C. NLG DOOR AND LINKAGE — SECURE.
   - D. LG/HOOK EMERGENCY PNEUMATIC BOTTLE — CHARGED.

SOURCE:
U.S. AIR FORCE MANUAL
T.O. 1F-16A-1

This Egyptian Air Force F-16A the has the larger horizontal stabilator introduced on late production block F-16As and standard on all later variants.

The F-16ADF variant is rapidly taking over the Air Defense mission from the F-4 Phantom II. The F-16ADF can easily be identified by the four blade antennas in front of the cockpit and on the bottom of the intake. The aircraft also has larger ECM bulges on the fin.

(Right) An F-16B of the 309th TFS, 31st TFW on the ramp at Homestead AFB, Florida. The F-16B is structurally the same as the F-16A and retains the same mission capability. Installation of the second seat costs some 1,200 pounds of internal fuel.

The nose of the F-16 mounts a number of sensors. There are two air data probes, one on the extreme nose and one just behind the radome. Additionally there is a TACAN blade antenna mounted under the nose to the rear of the radome.

(Left) The pilot and crew chief of this F-16 have begun the pre-flight walkaround, checking the aircraft for any possible problems that can be visually detected. This walkaround inspection is performed before each flight.

The spike-like object is the angle of attack (AOA) probe (one on each side) and the tear drop fairing covers one of the RHAWS (Radar Homing and Warning Sensor) antennas (again on both sides).

The static ports, just below the cockpit and just in front of the wing forestrake are circled in Red. The RESCUE arrow points to a push in door that contains a canopy jettison cable. The instructions for use of the cable are painted on the fuselage just to the left of the door . The aircraft's crew chief has his name painted on the fuselage just below the cockpit.

The Red ejection seat warning triangle is one of the few markings on this low vis camouflaged F-16C that is in full and bright color. The canopy on the F-16C is tinted to cut down on glare and make objects (and other aircraft) easier to see.

The open panel on this F-16C of the 57th FWW Aggressors allows access to the external power receptacle plug. The Red, outlined in Yellow, aircraft number is in the style used on Eastern European aircraft .The position light forward of the 71 is Green while the position light on the port side is Red.

The box with six prongs on the right is the plug in for the external power source. The switches to the left allow power to be transferred from the external power source to the aircraft's systems. This Viper carries the badge of the 57th FWW just to the rear of the open access panel.

European F-16A variants have two blade antennas mounted on the lower fuselage just behind the air intake. One antenna is an IFF antenna and the other is a TACAN antenna.

This F-16A is flown by the Belgian Air Force and has a UHF Identification Friend or Foe (IFF) blade antenna and a TACAN antenna mounted on the lower fuselage just behind the intake.

The canopy of an F-16C in the fully open position. The hook shaped objects on the canopy rail are the canopy locking latches. The canopy is a one piece bubble and is resistant to bird strikes.

The rescue marking are plainly visible on this F-16C. the two Red circles on the nose are static intakes, while the spike like object on the radome is an air data probe for the Angle of Attack (AOA) sensor.

The canopy of the F-16D is, like the single seater, a single piece bubble. The hydraulic canopy riser is located between the cockpits with the piston being located just behind the forward ejection seat.

Like the single seat F-16C, the F-16D canopy has grab handles that help the pilots maneuver their bodies during air combat maneuvering and also help in securing the canopy in the locked position.

The port side of the F-16 contains the external canopy open/close controls in the underside of the wing forestrake. The open access door has the squadron insignia painted on it in full color.

The nose of an F-16A reveals one of the principle visual differences between the F-16A and F-16C, the size and shape of the Head Up Display (HUD). The camera is behind the HUD in the F-16A and in front of the HUD in the F-16C.

This overall White F-16A of the 6512th Test Squadron at Edwards AFB has the rescue markings in full color and the unit badge on the fuselage just behind the canopy.

The boarding ladder hooks over the cockpit wall and has a brace that rests against the fuselage to steady the ladder. The Black and Red bag on the ladder contains the aircraft's documents. This F-16C was assigned to the 57th Fighter Weapons Wing at Nellis AFB, NV, during April of 1992.

The documents bag has the aircraft's serial number on it in Yellow. This bag contains the aircraft's maintenance logs and other important documents. The pilot assigned to this aircraft has his name painted on the canopy rail in Medium Gray.

The YF-16A had yet another canopy configuration. This aircraft had a camera mounted behind the Stencel SIIIS ejection seat, which was replaced on production F-16s with the Aces II seat.

The M61 Vulcan cannon port on a F-16A differs from the port on the later F-16C in the number of vents in front of and behind the port.

The crew chief of this F-16C has applied the insignia of the 64th Aggressor Squadron to the inside of one of the hydraulic accuator access doors.

This F-16A of the 157th TFS Swamp Foxes, of the S.C. Air National Guard carries a Outstanding Unit Award ribbon painted on the fuselage side.

The M61 cannon port on this F-16C of the 57th Fighter Weapons Wing has two vents behind the port while the F-16A cannon port has four vents.

This open access panel is for the ground power receptacle plug in on the F-16C. The power plug is inserted into the black box on the lower right.

The Armament panel above the small air scoop on this F-16C is empty, indicating that the aircraft is in an unarmed status. The aircraft carries the insignia of the F-16 Fighter Weapons School on the port side of fuselage.

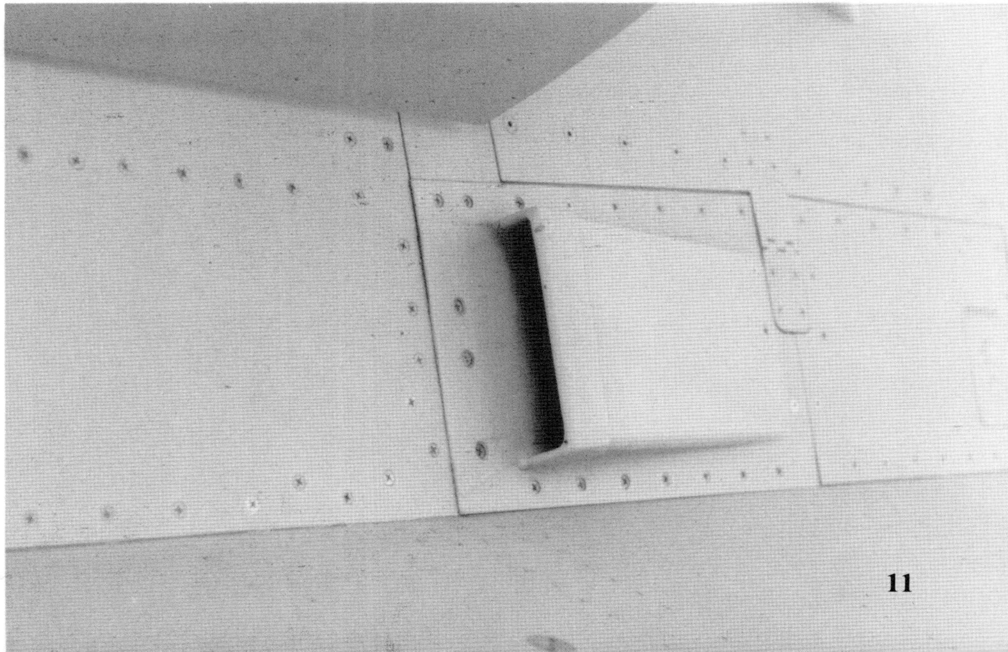

This rectangular air intake is located on the lower port side of the fuselage just under the wing trailing edge.

The HUD on this F-16 is covered with a Red protective cover. On either side of the canopy rail are two wire grab handles used by the pilot to pull the canopy down. The Red covers on either side of the nose are protective covers for the AOA air data probes.

The two rectangular wire objects on the canopy are the grab handles used by the pilot to lower the canopy and are also used to help him maneuver his body during air combat maneuvering. There are four hook shaped locking lugs on each side of the canopy sill.

The threat warning radar antenna fairing on the vertical fin of the F-16A is about half the size of the same antenna on the F-16C, making the position light appear to be lower on the fin.

The ECM threat warning radar antenna fairing on the F-16C is much larger than the same antenna carried on the F-16A. The light just below the fairing is a White position light.

This F-16A of the Texas Air National Guard has an enlarged ECM antenna fairing at the base of the vertical stabilizer. The aircraft has been painted with a special scheme to denote the unit's 75th anniversary.

This F-16C of the 57th Fighter Weapons Wing is painted in a special aggressor paint scheme known as the MiG-29 scheme The F-16C has a much larger horizontal stabilizer than the early F-16A (the new stabilator was introduced on Block 15 F-16As).

There is a small ram air scoop on the underside of the wing forestrake just below the cannon port on this F-16C.

The small bare metal L shaped ram air intake below is visible on the underside of the wing forestrake just above the Red 71 on the air intake and just above and behind the position light

This ram air scoop is located on the underside of the wing forestrake just under the M61 cannon port and is present on the F-16C/D only.

This small L shaped bare metal ram air scoop is located under the wing forestrake just above the air intake.

14

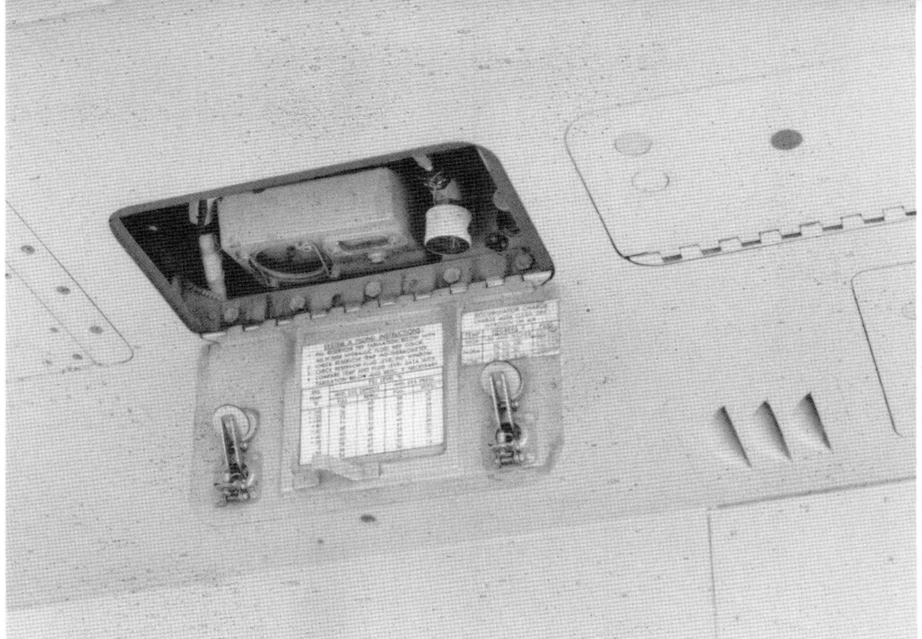

This is the Hydraulic System A filler access panel, located on the underside of the wing forestrake behind door # 3216.

This "egg crate" is the chaff/flare dispenser on an F-16A. The F-16C has two such dispensers on each side of the fuselage. The open access panel next to it is for checking the flight control accumulator.

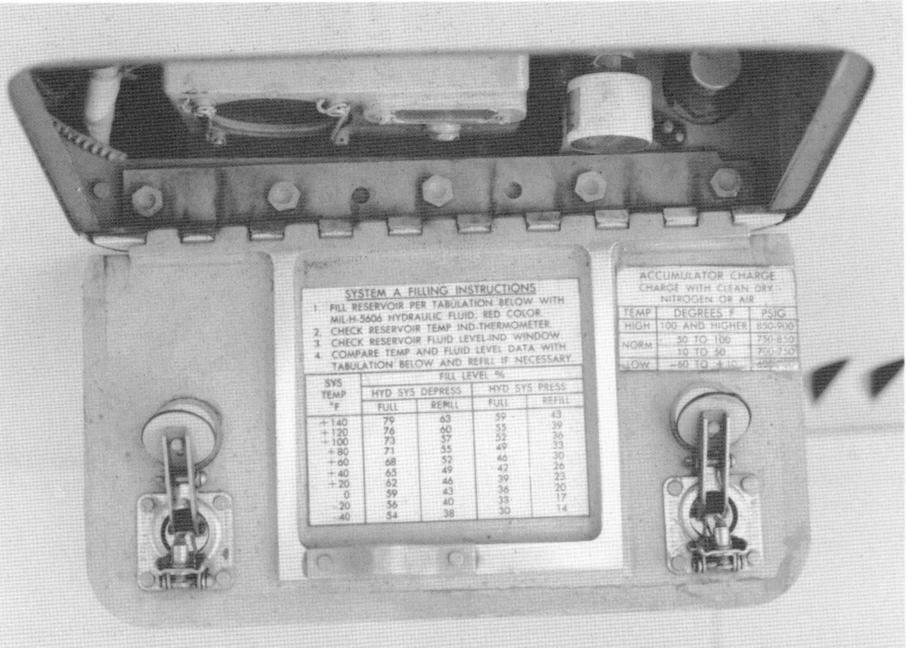

SYS TEMP °F	FILL LEVEL %			
	HYD SYS DEPRESS		HYD SYS PRESS	
	FULL	REFILL	FULL	REFILL
+140	79	63	59	43
+120	76	60	55	39
+100	73	57	52	36
+80	71	55	49	33
+60	68	52	46	30
+40	65	49	42	26
+20	62	46	39	23
0	59	43	36	20
-20	56	40	33	17
-40	54	38	30	14

TEMP	DEGREES F	PSIG
HIGH	100 AND HIGHER	850-900
NORM	50 TO 100	750-850
	10 TO 50	700-750
LOW	-60 TO +10	

The filling instructions for the Hydraulic System A are printed on the inside of the access panel door for servicing personnel.

The Auxiliary Power Unit (APU) exhaust door is discolored from the heat of the APU's exhaust. The APU is located on the underside of the fuselage just to the rear of the main landing gear and just forward of the ventral fin.

The underside of the right mid-wing root contains the access panel for the Hydraulic System Ground Power Connection and Reservoir.

The field arresting hook is carried on the aircraft centerline between the two ventral fins. The blade antenna on the right is normally hidden by the ventral fin and cannot be seen from the side.

The port position light on the intake of the F-16C is Red. The aircraft is carrying the insignia of the 432nd Tactical Fighter Wing in a Black outline form, which is common on low vis camouflaged aircraft.

Part of the pre-flight inspection is the landing gear wheel wells, tires and the landing gear itself. They are inspected for visual signs of fluid leaks along with excessive wear.

Another of the areas visually checked is the ventral fin and the field arresting hook which is mounted on the underside of the fuselage between the fins.

The starboard speed brake is fully open while the port speed brake is fully closed, while both horizontal stabilators are full down. The aircraft is also carrying a travel pod on the fuselage centerline station.

The partially opened speed brake on the starboard side of the F-16. On the ground, with no hydraulic power in the system, the speed brakes can be pried open manually.

The hydraulic piston located between the speed brake sissors both opens and closes the unit. The speed brakes can be operated in the full open position, full closed position or one of several intermediate positions.

The fully open speed brake reveals the lightening holes cut in the structure to help reduce the overall weight of the speed brake assembly.

The parachute harness/survival vest has a number of straps including two that pass between the legs and hook in front. These are one of the last things the pilot adjusts before boarding his aircraft.

While the aircraft's crew chief stands by, the pilot of this F-16C prepares to board his aircraft. He is adjusting his parachute harness which is worn over the survival vest. The Green bag on the ramp is his helmet carrying bag . The hose hanging from the left leg is the anti-G suit attachment hose.

With his helmet bag and flight bag in hand, the pilot climbs the boarding ladder, while the crew chief stands by ready to assist if needed. The last rung of the ladder does not reach the ground and there is about a one foot step up to reach the first rung.

When the pilot is finished with the pre-flight walkaround, he signs off on the 781 Form, noting any discrepancy with the aircraft. The best way to get into the tight cockpit of an F-16C is to sit on the top rung of the ladder (which forms a wide platform), insert your right leg, slide into the seat, and jackknife your left leg into the tunnel leading to the rudder pedal. This is guaranteed to keep you limber!

The latest production variant of the F-16C has two double head lamp style landing lights installed on the inside of the nose gear door, because the FLIR pods blocked out the lights installed in the main wheel well.

The nose gear on all F-16 variants is a fully steerable nose wheel which rotates thirty-two degrees left/right around the center of the strut.

The nose gear door on the F-16A does not have landing lights installed on the door. The interior of the wheel well and door are White to help detect fluid leaks.

The piston to the right of the nose wheel is the nose wheel well door retraction arm. The names of the aircraft's maintenance crew are carried on the inside of the gear door in Black.

The nose landing gear is an oleo type strut with rear scissors. The nose wheel is fully steerable being activated via the rudder pedals.

The F-16C nose wheel is an oleo type strut with a rear scissors. The strut running back into the wheel well from the middle of the nose wheel strut is the retraction arm.

The F-16 has a steerable nose wheel which rotates around the middle of the strut. The oval shaped housing on the front of the strut is the nose wheel steering control.

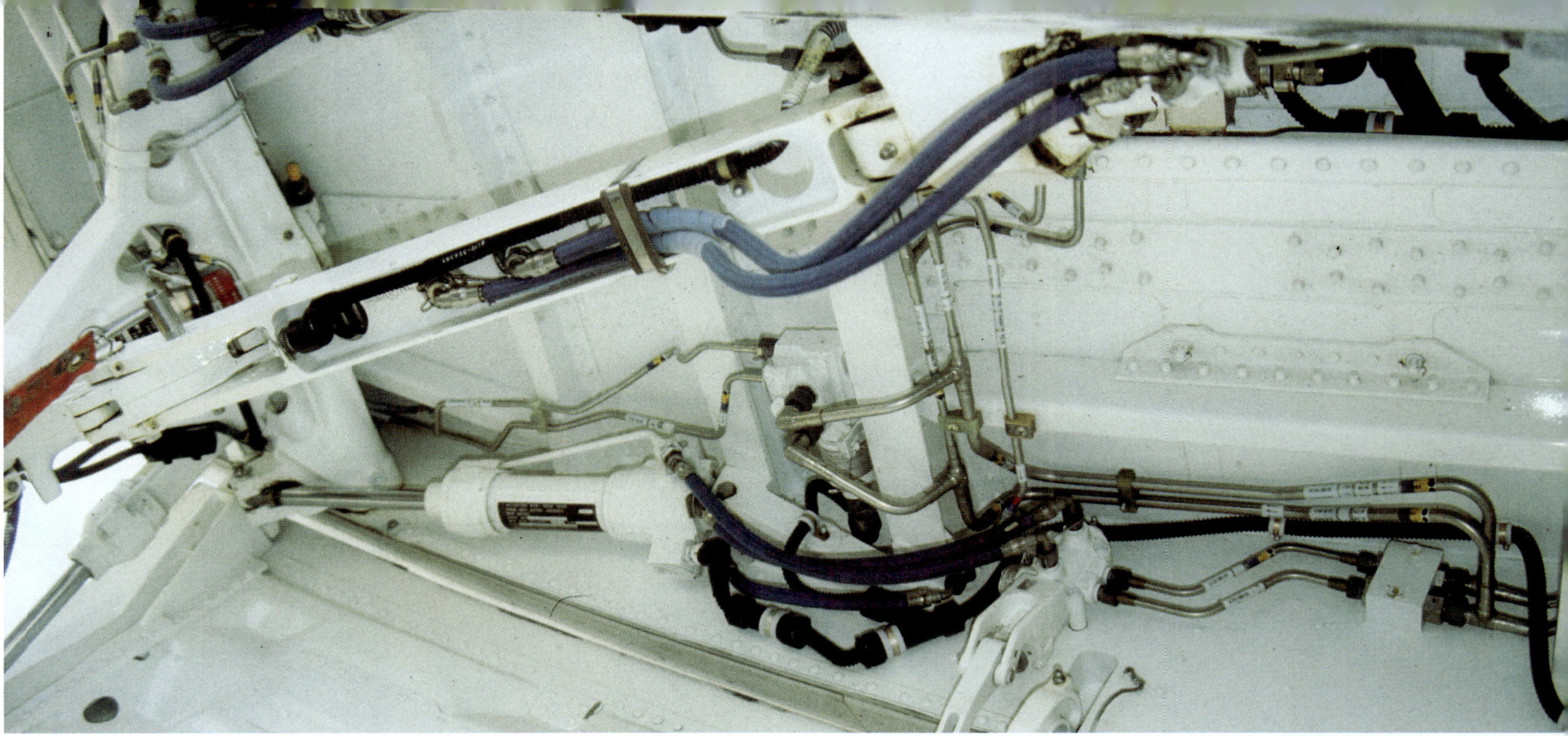

The interior of the nose wheel well is full of various lines including pneumatic and hydraulic lines. The piston at the lower left is the gear door retraction arm. while the piston behind it is the wheel retraction control arm.

NOSE WHEEL WELL

The interior of the wheel well, wheel well door and landing gear struts are all painted in Gloss White to aid in the detection of hydraulic fluid leaks. The names of the aircraft's maintenance crew are carried on the inside of the nose wheel door in Black.

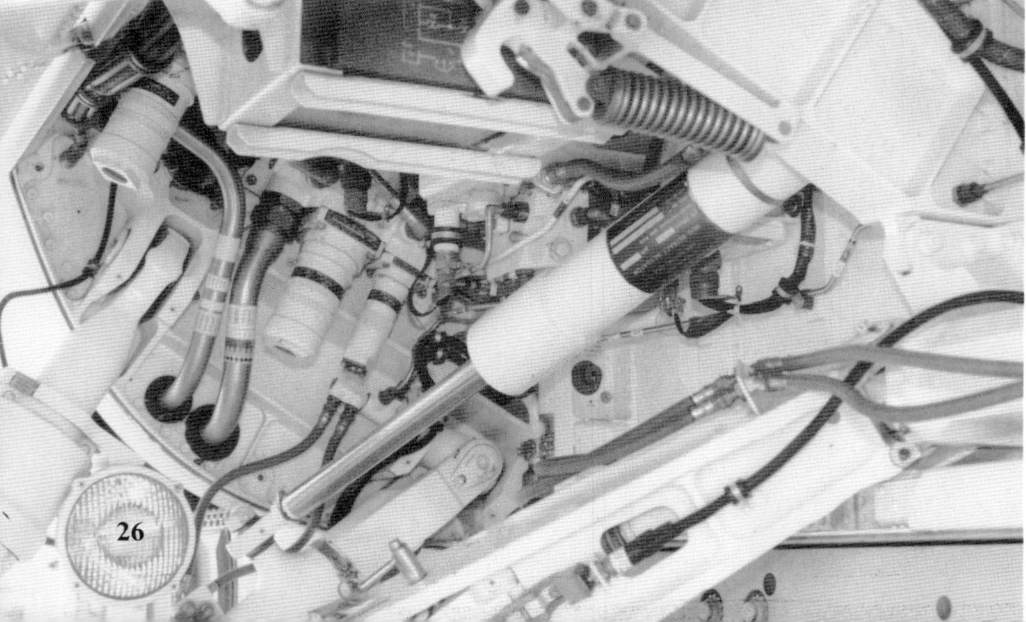

The Black lines running down the inboard main landing gear strut are part of the F-16's anti-skid system.

The starboard main landing gear has a taxi light installed between the landing gear struts. The piston is the landing gear retraction arm. The main gear retracts forward.

The field arresting hook on the F-16 is installed on the fuselage centerline just to the rear of the main landing gear wheel wells. The open access panel reveals one of the engine accessory bays.

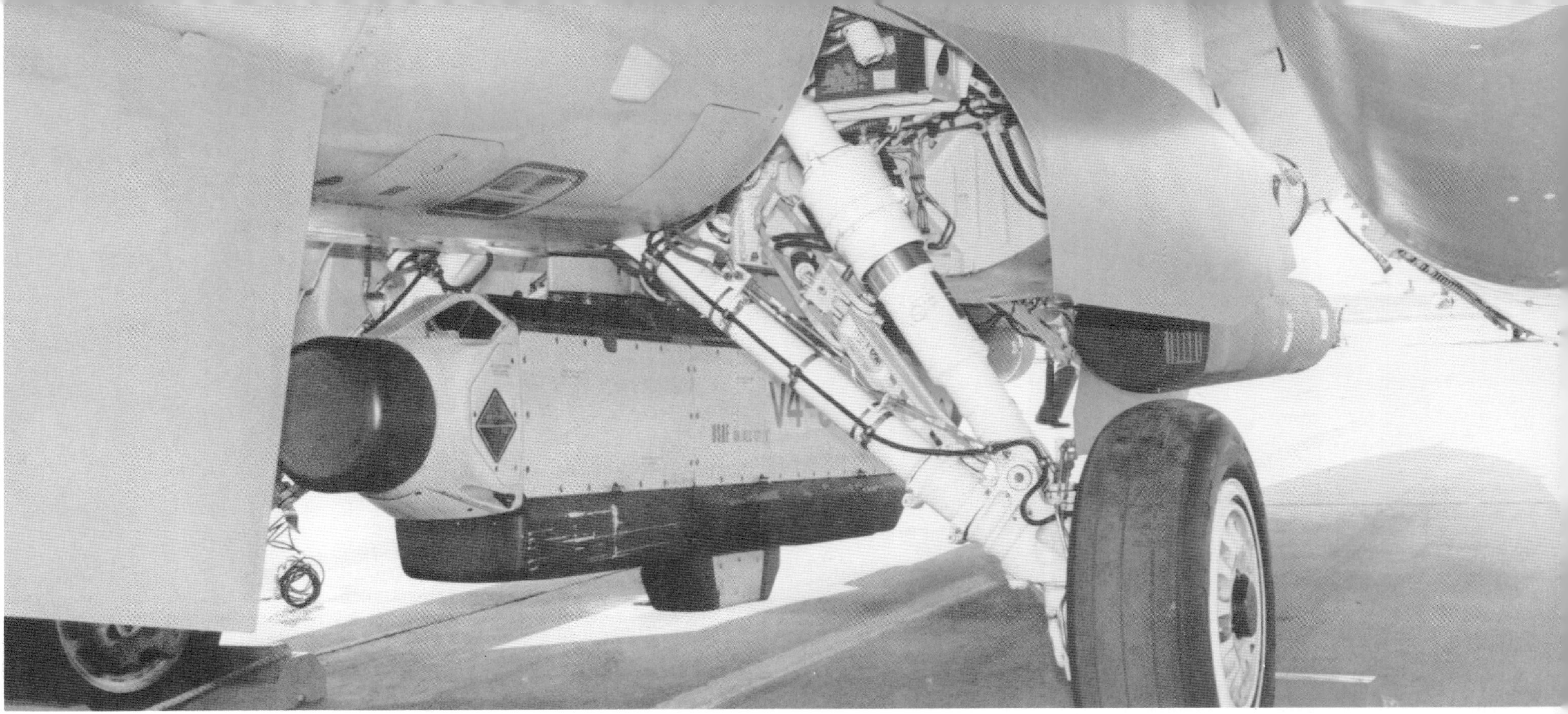

The ECM pod on the centerline station is an ALQ-131 pod, one of the more widely used jammer pods in the USAF inventory.

The main wheels and brakes on the F-16C are made by Goodyear and the tires are made by B.F. Goodrich. The main gear has ten locking lugs.

A ground crewmen checks the starboard main landing gear wheel well hydraulic door piston and immediate area for signs of fluid leaks or other damage.

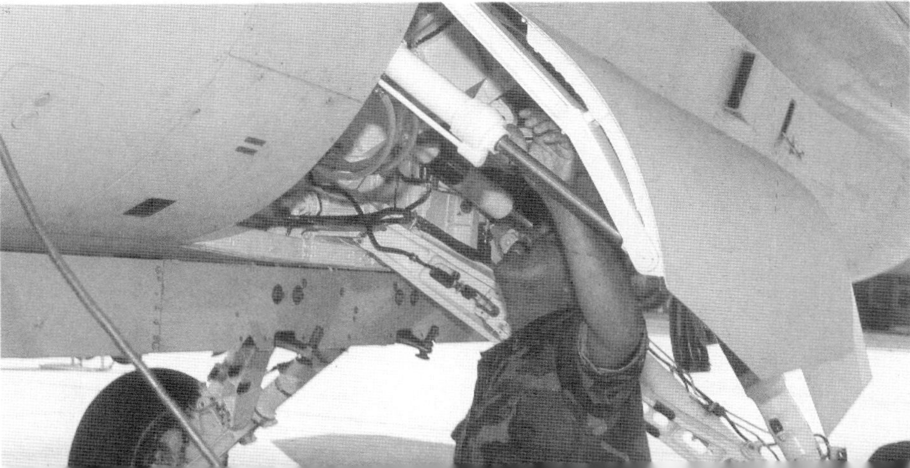

The access panel that the pilot is checking is the inspection port for the Liquid Oxygen (LOX) system. This is located behind access door #3308.

Just in front of the main landing gear wheel well on the port side of the aircraft is a painted box labeled Armament. This section of the fuselage is used by the armament crew to note the weapons loaded on the aircraft (if any).

The piston above the pilots head is the main landing gear door retraction arm. The retraction of all gear doors is hydraulic. Visual inspection of the gear wells is important to detect fluid leaks.

The port main landing gear mount on an F-16C. The steel lines running down the inboard strut to the wheel are brake lines which supply hydraulic fluid to the main wheel brakes.

The Black lines running down the inboard landing gear strut are part of the F-16's anti-skid and wheel speed sensor system. The wheel speed sensor system halts the moving main wheel before it is retracted into the wheel well. Each main wheel has ten locking lugs.

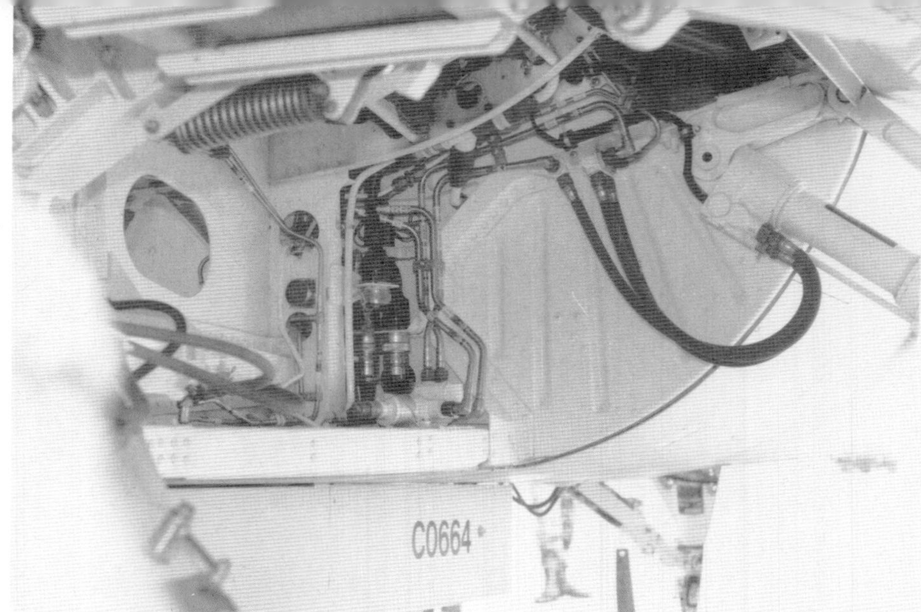

The landing gear well of the F-16C has a number of different hydraulic lines running through it, some are part of the anti-skid system and others are brake lines.

The open access panel behind the ventral fin is the Wheel Brake Pneumatic Reservoir and the one in front of it is the Engine Oil Sight Gage The circle on fuel tank is the filler port.

The F-16 has hydraulic anti-lock brakes on each main wheel. Many of the landing gear components are interchangeable from port to starboard.

Servicing Diagram

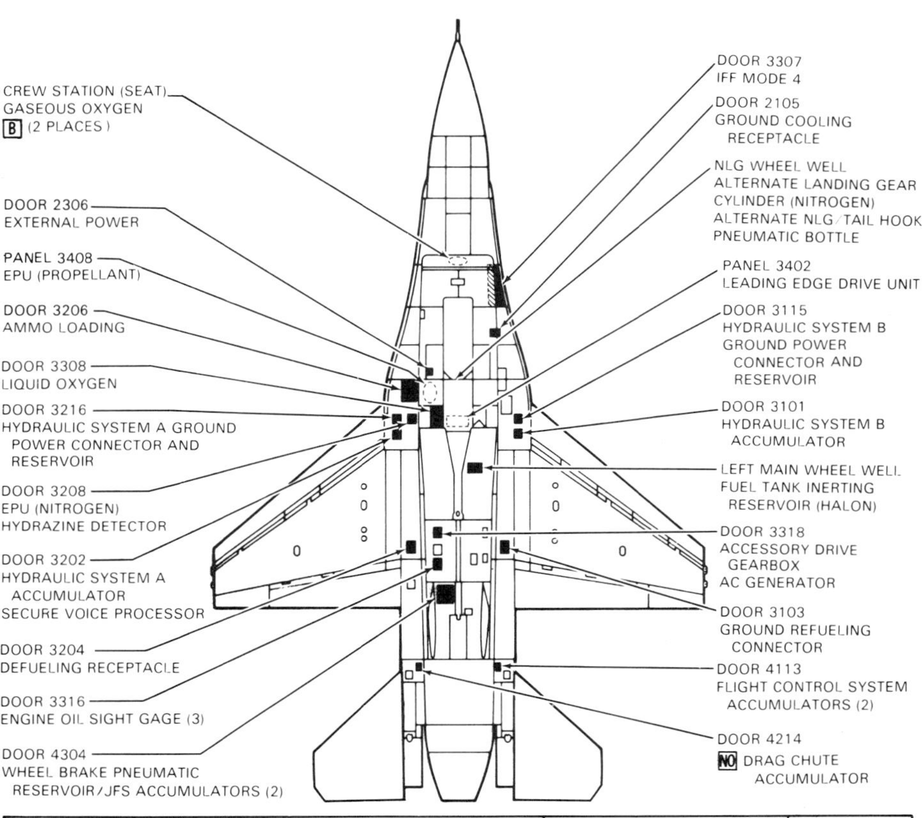

SPECIFICATIONS		USAF	NATO
FUEL	PRIMARY	MIL-T-5624, JP-4	F-40
	ALTERNATE (REFER TO SECTION V)	MIL-T-83133, JP-8 ASTM, JET A-1 (COMMERCIAL) ASTM, JET B (COMMERCIAL)	F-34 F-35
OIL	TURBINE ENGINE ACCESSORY DRIVE GEARBOX	MIL-L-7808	O-148
HYDRAULIC FLUID		MIL-H-5606	H-515
OXYGEN	LIQUID	MIL-O-27210, TYPE II	NONE
	GASEOUS	MIL-O-27210, TYPE I	NONE
EXTERNAL ELECTRICAL POWER	115 ± 15 VAC, 400 ± 30 Hz	A/M 32A-60A	NONE
NITROGEN	GASEOUS	BB-N-411a TYPE I GRADE B	NONE
FUEL TANK INERTING AGENT	LIQUID	HALON 1301	NONE
MONOPROPELLANT (EPU)	LIQUID	HYDRAZINE (N2H4) (70-30%)	NONE

SOURCE:
U.S. AIR FORCE MANUAL
T.O. 1F-16A-1

Antenna Locations

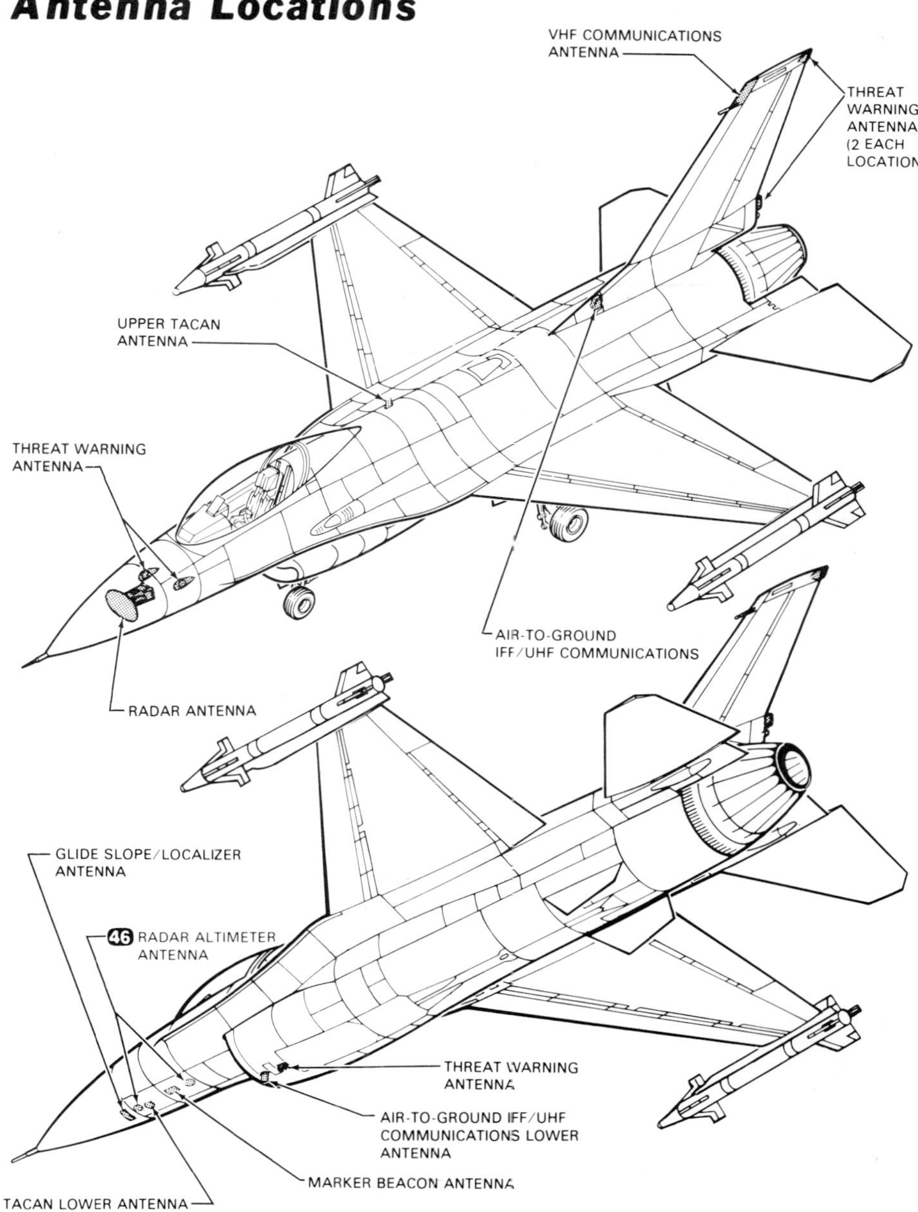

SOURCE:
U.S. AIR FORCE MANUAL
T.O. 1F-16A-1

The pod mounted on the centerline station is an ALQ-131 ECM jammer pod .This pod was carried on most F-16Cs engaged in attack missions during Operation DESERT STORM. The main landing gear of the F-16 retracts foward. The aircraft is equipped with a wheel speed sensor that automatically stops the spinning wheel before it enters the wheel well.

A taxi light is located between the landing gear struts. The piston at the top left is the main gear door retraction arm. As with the nose gear strut, the main landing gear struts are oleo type struts.

This F-16C of the 57th FWW is carrying a travel pod under the starboard wing. Travel pods are used to carry the pilots personal luggage on cross country flights to distant bases.

The F-16 is equipped with a high pressure single point refueling system and this port is the plug-in.

The open access panels on the starboard lower fuselage of the F-16C are (from front to rear) the Accessory Drive gearbox, engine oil sight gage and wheel brake pneumatic reservoir.

This F-16C of the 57th Fighter Weapons Wing is the latest production variant of the F-16 and is equipped with LANTIRN/FLIR pods on either side of the intake.

Norwegian Air F-16As were the first to feature the longer base to the vertical fin and a braking parachute. This was necessary due the harsh winter conditions in Norway.

This F-16A of the Royal Norwegian Air Force carries additional antenna fairings on either side of the braking parachute housing at the base of the vertical fin.

The braking parachute is used by countries that have a large number of air bases with short or unimproved runways.

The braking parachute housing is located at the base of the vertical fin on Belgian F-16As. Most F-16 variants do not use a braking parachute, relying on aerodynamic braking after landing to bleed off speed.

A pair of maintenance men work on engine connections in the engine bay of an F-16C. There is no need for special stands or other work stands to do routine maintenance on the F-16. The interior of the engine bay is painted Zink chromate Yellow.

The engine bay on the F-16C was designed to be easily accessible from ground level, making it possible to do engine maintenance without special work stands. This greatly enhances the aircraft's ability to deploy to remote bases.

Maintenance personnel work on equipment in the engine bay of an F-16C of the 57th Fighter Weapon Wing. With no hydraulic pressure, the field arrestor hook has settled into the full down position.

The maintenance dolly is used to remove the Pratt and Whitney F-100 engine from the F-16 and to transport it. Most engine work can be performed while the engine is safely secured on the maintenance dolly.

This F-16C is powered by a Pratt & Whitney F100-PW-200 turbofan engine. The starboard speed brake is in the fully open position while the port speed brake is closed.

This bay, located behind the port main landing gear wheel well, contains the engine fuel controls and other engine auxiliary equipment.

This F-16C with its Pratt & Whitney engine in the full open position, was assigned to the 363rd Fighter Wing, at Shaw Air Force Base, S.C. during June of 1992.

The jet exhaust on this General Electric powered F-16C is in the fully closed or idle power position.

The pre-production F-16 vertical fin lacked the threat warning antenna fairing at the base of the rudder, having only a position light.

The F-16A has a smaller threat warning radar antenna fairing at the base of the fin than the F-16C, which makes the position light appear lower down on the fin. This F-16A is assigned to the New York Air National Guard.

The jet exhaust of the General Electric F-110-GE-100 turbofan engine in fully open (afterburner) position. This is an F-16C with the larger RHAW antenna fairing at the base of the rudder.

The exhaust vanes on the engine are known as "Turkey Feathers" and those of the Pratt & Whitney F-100 engine differ slightly from those of the GE engine.

The exhaust vanes are fully open on this F-16C. The F-16C uses two different engines (either a P&W F110-PW-200 or General Electric F110 power plant) depending on what production block the aircraft comes from.

The F-16N is based on the airframe of the F-16C and is powered by the General Electric F110 turbofan engine. This F-16N carries the insignia of the Navy Fighter Weapons School (TOPGUN) on the fin.

The starboard speed brake on this F-16C is partially open. Without hydraulic pressure the speed brakes often open on their own.

The port speed brake on this F-16 is fully closed while the port stabilator is in the full down position. It is not uncommon to see F-16s parked on the ramp with the stabilator's in this position.

Exterior Lighting

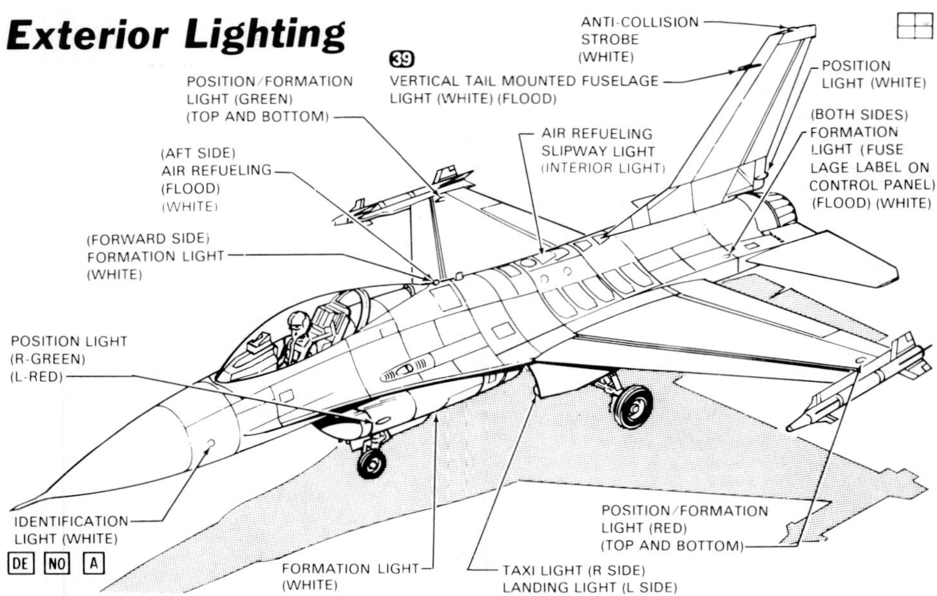

The F-16Cs tail has a small air scoop and blade antenna on the fin leading edge. This F-16C belongs to 512th TFS, 86th TFW at Ramstein Air Base, Germany. Its exhaust identifies it as a GE engined Viper.

The F-16As tail has a number of differences between it and the F-16C including a smaller ECM antenna fairing. The lines coming off the trailing edge of the fin and rudder are static electricity discharge wicks.

This F-16BADF variant of the 159th FIS, Florida Air National Guard has a searchlight on the nose for night identification of aircraft in the Air Defense Identification Zone (ADIZ) mounted under the RHAW antenna cover.

The "turkey feathers" on this Pratt & Whitney F-100 engine are fully opened for periodic maintenance. The engine is resting on an engine test stand that is used to remove the engine from the F-16.

A Pratt & Whitney F-100 engine being run at full power in the engine test cell at Springfield, Illinois. Engines are put through tests such as this before being reinstalled in F-16.

A compact and powerful Pratt & Whitney F-100 turbofan engine on an engine test stand. The engine suffered teething problems, but its light weight and high performance has kept it at the forefront of fighter engines for nearly two decades.

The General Electric J-79 was a highly successful engine, powering all U.S. F-4 Phantoms and the F-16/79 demonstrator. It was rated at 17,000 lbst, was 18 inches longer than the F-100 engine (24,000 lbst) and required 2,000 pounds of heat shielding. The F16/79 was not successful and was never built.

This "big mouth" F-16C is equipped with the LANTIRN navigation/attack system which is carried in two pods mounted on either side of the air intake. The LANTIRN F-16C first saw action during Operation DESERT STORM.

With an anti-FOD cover over the intake, a Pratt and Whitney F-100 engine rests on a maintenance dolly after it was removed from the engine bay of an F-16C. The lever on the side of the dolly is a hydraulic pump which moves the engine forward and back on the dolly.

The air intake on the F-16C is much larger than the intake on early F-16As and is known as the "big mouth" intake. There are two large lights mounted on the nose gear wheel well door.

The two LANTIRN FLIR pods allow the Viper to find and attack targets at night and in bad weather. This pod is the targeting FLIR pod which is carried on the starboard side of the intake.

The LANTIRN system consists of two pods; a Forward Looking Infrared (FLIR) navigation pod carried on the port side of the intake and a FLIR targeting pod carried on the starboard side.

The ram air intake at the rear of the LANTIRN FLIR targeting pod provides cooling air for the electronics systems within the pod. A similar air intake is also found on the FLIR navigation pod.

The Rapport III warning antenna/position light housing is visible on the intake of this F-16D of the IAD/AF.   F-16Cs and F-16Ds of the IDF/AF have also been modified with an enlarged spine which houses additional electronics.

The position lights on either side of the air intake on European F-16As have enlarged mountings which contain the Rapport III threat warning antenna. This antenna is found on Belgian and Israel Vipers.

A General Dynamics technician performs routine systems checks on one of the pre-production prototypes. The radome is off and the nose electronics bays are opened.

The cockpit of an F-16C Fighting Falcon. The Yellow handle just in front of the seat is the ejection handle. There are two Multi-Functional Display screens on either side of the center panel.

The TV display on an F-16D two seat proficiency trainer. The F-16B rear seat TV is shielded by a hood and the MFD screens are located directly under the HUD.

The Red Remove Before Flight flag is attached to the safety pin in the ejection seat safing lever. As long as this pin is in place the seat cannot be fired.

The Vipers night eyes are evident in this simulated LANTIRN HUD display, and FLIR display on the right MFD. This HUD was not selected for installation in the F-16. (General Dynamics)

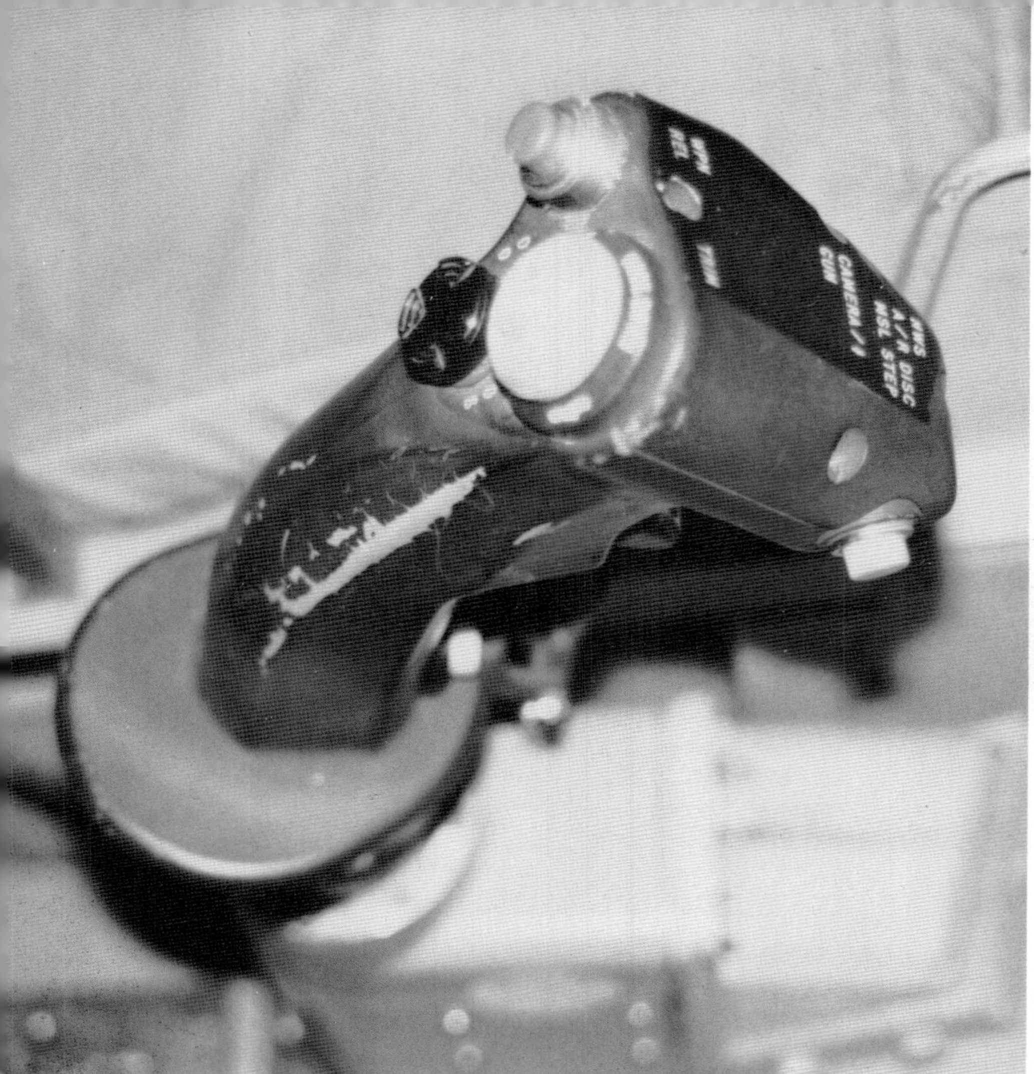

The sidestick controller of an F-16A. Visible on the sidestick are the trim button, weapons release button and air-to-air/air-to-ground designate switch.

The cockpit of an F-16A has the Head Up Display (HUD) control knobs directly under the HUD mount, with conventional instruments under them as an emergency backup. A Multi-Function Display (MFD) screen is to the left of the HUD.

This is the throttle of an F-16C with the throttle lock in place. The rectangular object at the right is the ejection seat safety, with its safety pin in place.

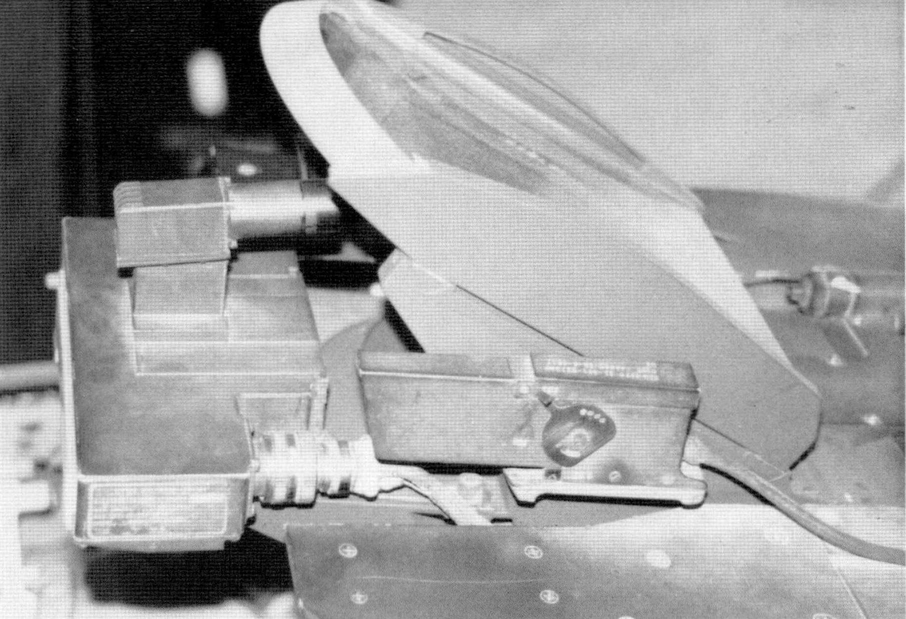

The HUD on the F-16A has the TV camera mounted to the rear of the HUD glass. The F-16C uses a different HUD with the TV camera in front of the HUD.

The rear portion of the F-16A canopy is fixed and the front bubble rotates over it. There are a number of electronic "black boxes" in the area behind the ejection seat.

The YF-16 prototypes were equipped with the Stencel SIIIS ejection seat, while all production F-16 variants use the Aces II ejection seat.

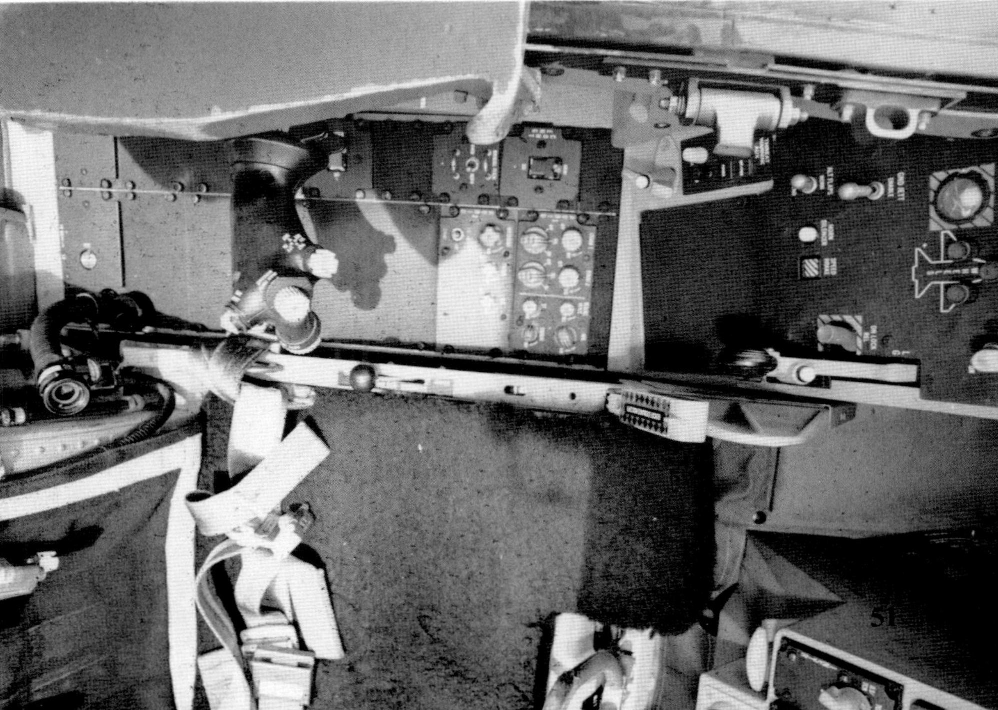

The port console in the front cockpit of the F-16D two seat proficiency trainer has the communications control panel immediately in front of the throttle.

Immediately below the HUD in this F-16N is the HUD control panel which contains all the push buttons used to both input and request data to be displayed on the HUD. The MFD screen to the left is the stores information screen.

The cockpit of an F-16C with the ejection seat removed. The number of various buttons and switches on the throttle show why modern fighter pilots spend a lot of time learning to "play the piccolo".

This is the Head Up Display (HUD) installed in the Navy F-16N. The F-16N is a special variant built for the Navy as a dissimilar air combat trainer. It carries no internal armament.

The Green bottle on the side of the seat is an emergency oxygen bottle which supplies the pilot with oxygen if he is forced to eject at high altitudes. the Black area on top of the headrest is the drogue parachute container.

Aces II Ejection Seat

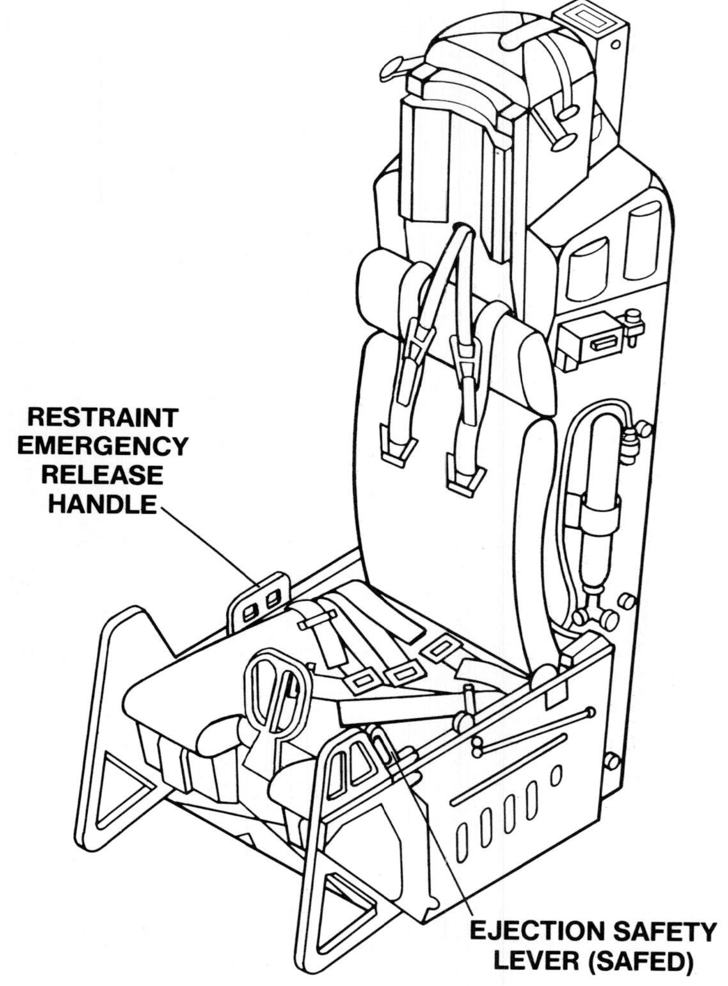

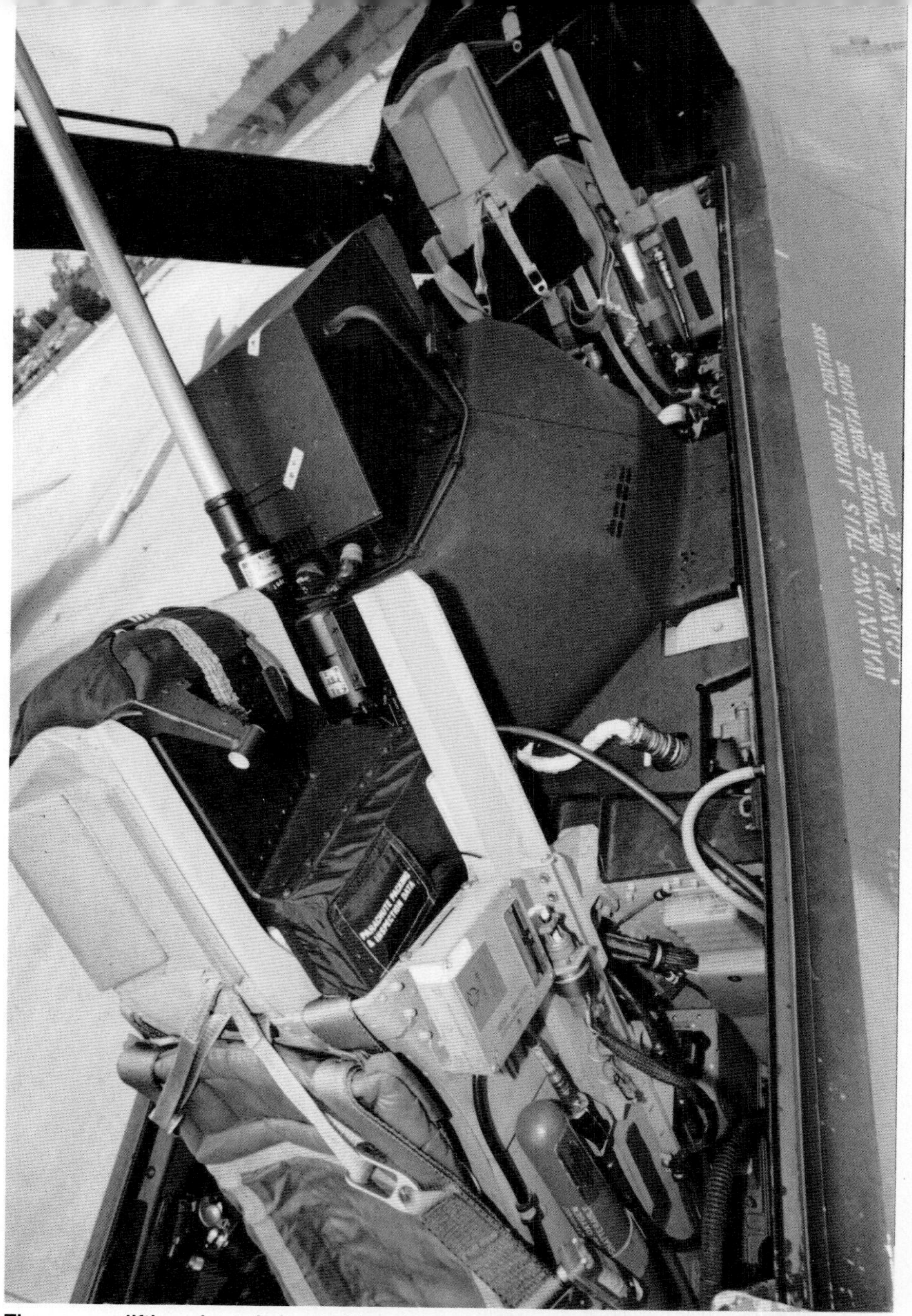

The canopy lifting piston is located just behind the front Aces II ejection seat in the F-16D. The rear cockpit contains TV screen on top the rear instrument panel, which repeats the information displayed on the front cockpit HUD.

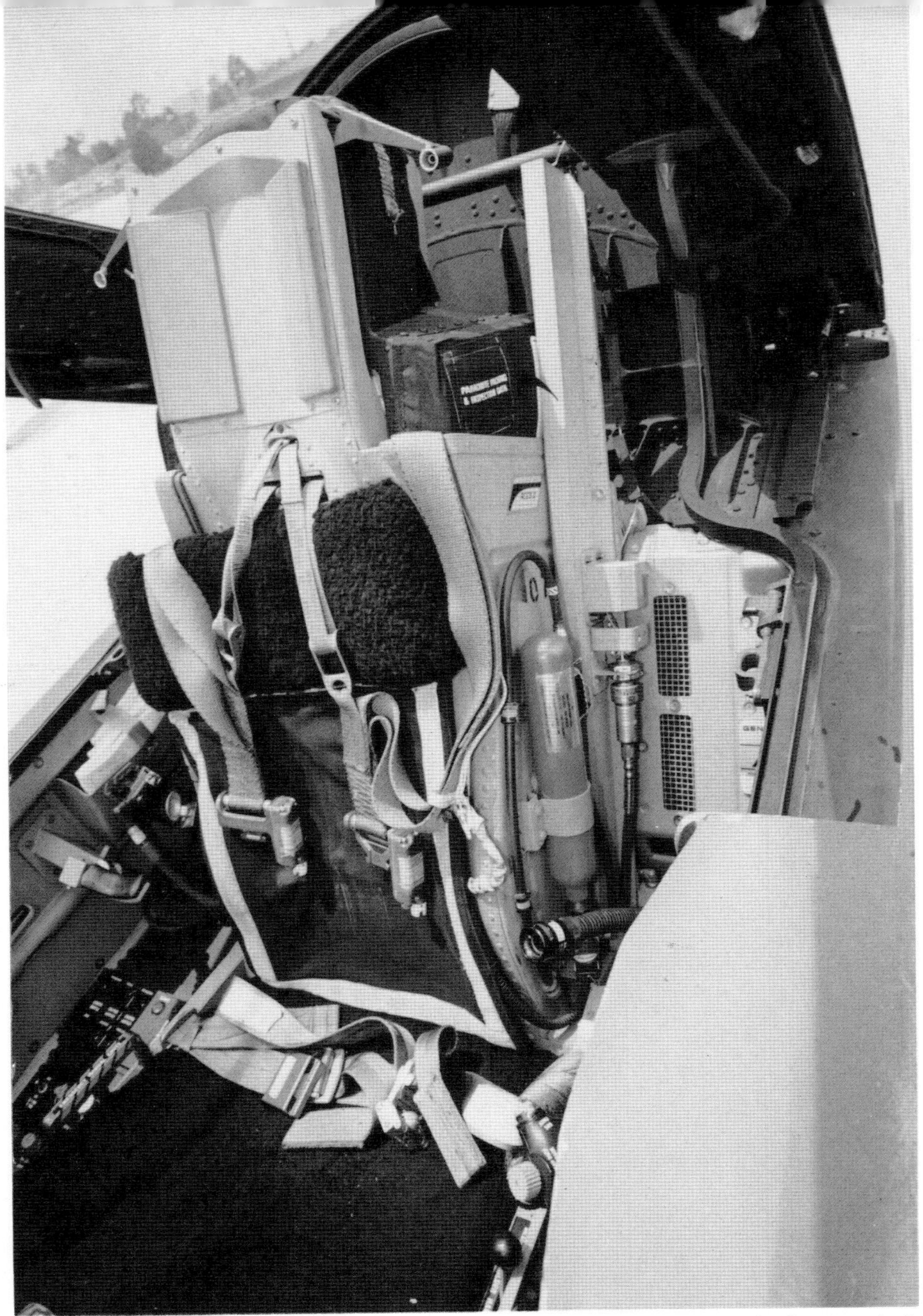

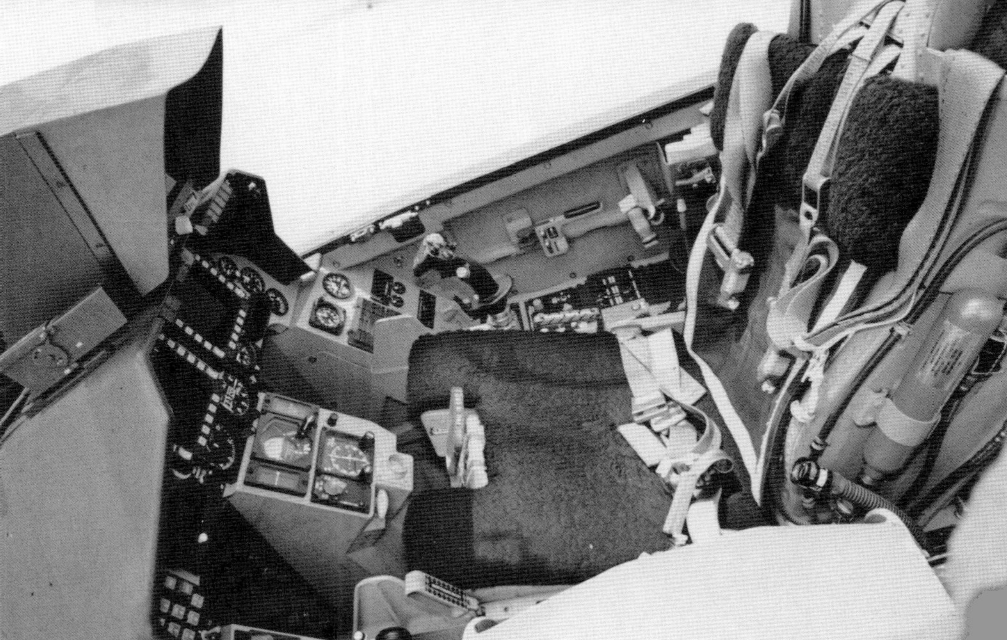

The rear cockpit of the F-16D is dominated by the shielded TV screen (which mirrors the front HUD display) and two Multi-Function Display screens directly under it. The Green bottle alongside the ejection seat is the emergency bail out Oxygen bottle.

This F-16 is undergoing periodic maintenance and has the canopy removed. The fixed clear panel behind the canopy is seldom removed unless it is necessary to gain access to some of the "black boxes" installed in this area.

The rear Aces II ejection seat in an F-16D is identical to the seat found in the front cockpit. The Aces II seat has a complex set of straps designed to hold the pilot securely to the seat in the event of an ejection.

The rear seat HUD repeats everything seen on the front cockpit HUD on the F-16D. The two MFD screens can be used to display a wide variety of information including stores data.

The two metal cylinders on the outside of the shoulder harness connectors are salt-water sensors. These will automatically cause the survival raft to inflate when they encounter salt water in the event of a water landing.

This F-16 pilot is using the lightweight HGU-55P flight helmet which is now standard issue for all USAF aircrews.

The ejection seat rests on these guide rails when installed in the cockpit of the F-16 Fighting Falcon.

The air-to-air refueling receptacle door is open as this F-16 moves into position to take on fuel from a KC-135 tanker. The markings ahead of the door are guides to assist the boom operator on the tanker.

The flaps on this F-16B are in the full down position. It is uncommon to see the flaps on the F-16 in the down position while the aircraft is on the ground.

The boom operator on a KC-135 makes contact with an F-16 and begins to transfer fuel to the fighter. The refueling port on the F-16 is located along the centerline of the aircraft spine.

The nose radome on this F-16A is folded back to reveal the Westinghouse APG-66 multi-function pulse Doppler radar. The open access doors behind the radar are electronics bays.

The radome is folded back and the electronics bay doors are opened and braced so technicians can perform maintenance on the multi-function APG-66 pulse Doppler radar and associated electronics on this F-16A.

Most of the electronics on the F-16 are modular and the aircraft is designed so that these components are readily accessible from ground level for ease of maintenance.

The radar antenna on the APG-66 is a flat phased array type of antenna. The electronics components in the compartment behind the radome have handles to allow them to be pulled out on built-in tracks for easy access.

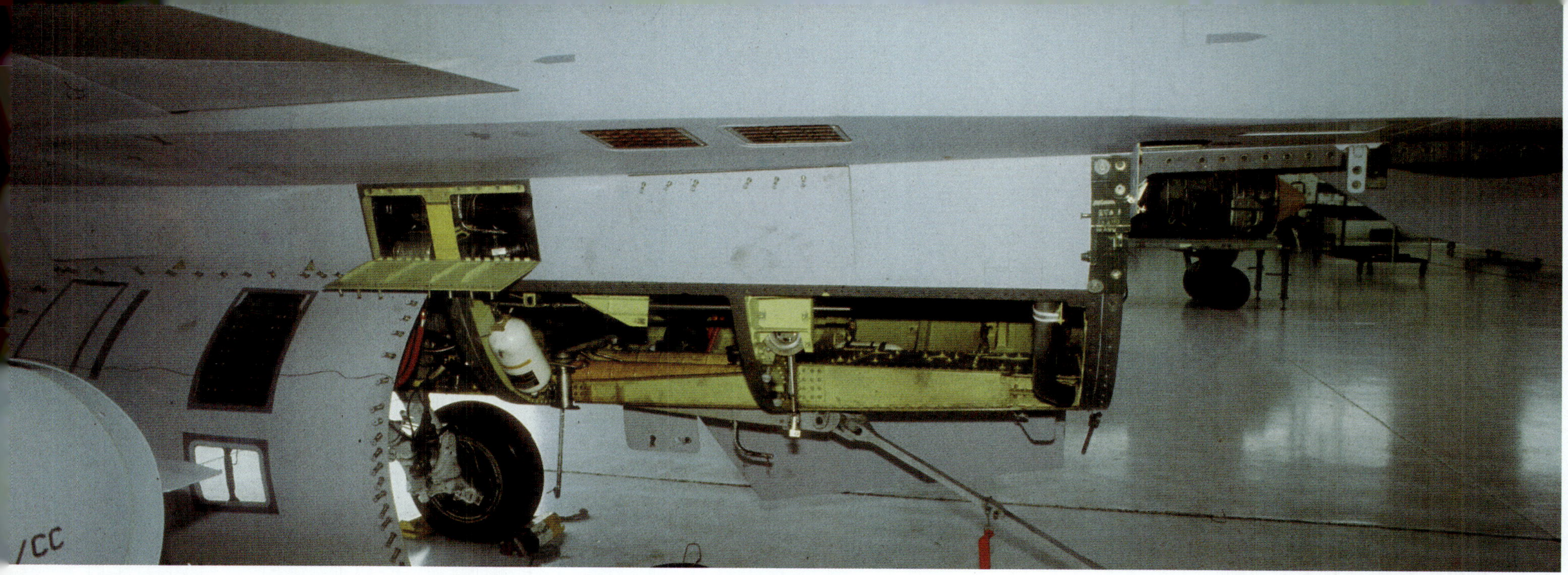

This F-16C is undergoing routine maintenance with the engine removed. The missing access panel also supports the left ventral fin. With the fin removed, the mounting of the field arrestor hook is visible.

AIRCRAFT MAINTENANCE

Access panels on the aircraft spine are also removed during periodic inspections. During these inspections, items needing replacement or repair are removed from the aircraft and serviced.

Most of the inspection panels are open on the F-16 as is undergoes periodic maintenance. The aircraft has an Outstanding Unit Award ribbon painted on the nose wheel door.

60

The light on the port landing gear strut of the F-16A and F-16B is designated as a landing light, while a similar light on the starboard landing gear leg is designated as a taxi light.

During inspections panels are removed and placed on the fuselage nearby. After the maintenance crew completes their inspection/repair as necessary, the panel is replaced.

This panel immediately behind the main landing gear well contains engine accessory equipment.

This mini-crane is used by maintenance personnel to remove the canopy and ejection seat from the F-16 for routine maintenance.

Large Red safety covers are in place over the Angel of Attack (AOA) air data probes on the radome of this F-16 to protect them while the aircraft is undergoing routine maintenance. The weight suspended from the nose is to compensate for the missing ejection seat.

A maintenance technician inspects the field arresting hook on this F-16 as it undergoes periodic inspection/major maintenance. The engine has been removed from this Viper.

Periodic inspections and major maintenance opens most inspection/access panels including these on the lower port fuselage.

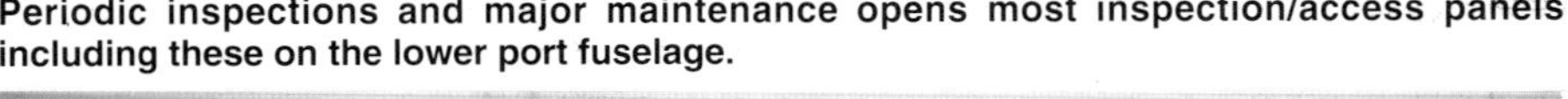

This lowered access panel is for the circuit breaker panel which is located under the starboard wing leading edge extension.

This open access panel is located immediately in front of the main landing gear well and contains hydraulic lines and sight gages.

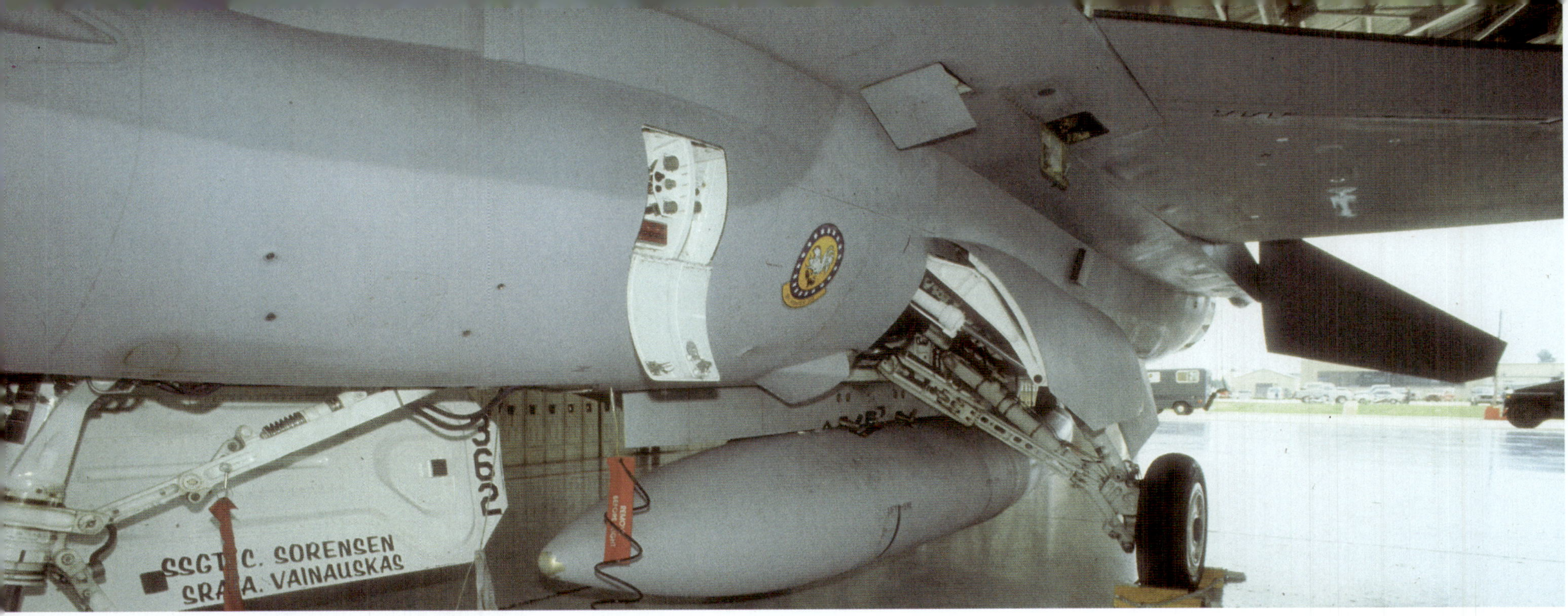

The Black coil line running from the aircraft is an electrical ground cable, which is connected to the aircraft during maintenance to bleed off any static electricity. This aircraft is carrying a 300 gallon centerline fuel tank.

The two open access panels under the leading edge of the wing extension are the inspection panels for the hydraulic system and the nitrogen system.

The skinning on the vertical tail fin has been removed to allow maintenance of the supporting structure of this F-16A. The aircraft also has the engine removed.

This is an external power cart used with the F-16 and other USAF jet aircraft.

The power cords are stored on top of the cart when not in use. The rectangular box below the cart is the fuel tank and it displays prominent safety markings.

The front panel on the external power cart has all the operating and safety instruction plainly displayed below the operating switches and dials.

This maintenance technician is preparing to load Liquid Oxygen (LOX) into the LOX tank on an F-16C at Nellis Air Force Base during April of 1993.

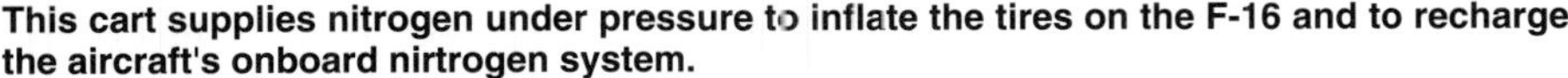

This cart supplies nitrogen under pressure to inflate the tires on the F-16 and to recharge the aircraft's onboard nirtrogen system.

This small battery cart is used to supply DC current to the aircraft so that ground crews can perform some of the necessary ground checks on the aircratt.

Nitrogen is used to inflate the tires on the F-16 because nirtogen, unlike compressed air, does not expand when the aircraft is at altitude.

This generator cart supplies all the electrical power needed to perform systems checks on all the F-16's avionics and is also used to help start the engine.

Large chemical fire extinguishers are kept on the flight line to handel any small fires that might erupt from spilt fuel or electrical short circuits.

Ground crews have attached a hose from a portable air conditioning unit to this F-16A to keep the aircraft's avionics cool while the crew performs ground checks.

The 370 gallon underwing fuel tank is rated as a supersonic tank. This tank is mounted on the inboard wing station of a LANTIRN equipped F-16C.

This is an MJ-1 power bomb loader used ot load weapons onto the wing pylons of USAF tactical aircraft, such as the F-16.

The standard underwing fuel tank for the F-16 is a 370 gallon tank that is carried on the inboard wing station. The Red circle on top of the tank is the filler cap.

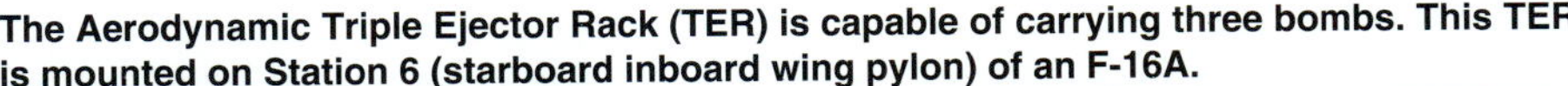

The Aerodynamic TER used on the F-16 has much less drag than the earlier Triple Ejector Rack used on Vietnam era tactical fighters such as the F-4 Phantom II and F-105 Thunderchief.

Armament crews use a power bomb loader to load CBU-87 cluster bombs onto the Aerodynamic TER on the outboard wing pylon of an F-16C during Operation DESERT STORM.

The Aerodynamic Triple Ejector Rack (TER) is capable of carrying three bombs. This TER is mounted on Station 6 (starboard inboard wing pylon) of an F-16A.

The standard under fuselage fuel tank is a 300 gallon supersonic tank. The tank is carried on the centerline station on all F-16 variants.

This crew travel pod is suspended from staion 7 (outboard port pylon) . The travel pod is used to carry crew belongings on cross country flights or on deployments away from home base.

The line running from this 370 gallon underwing fuel tank is a grounding wire which is attached during all fueling operations. The circular objects on top the tank are filler ports.

These servicing markings are carried on the 370 gallon underwing fuel tanks carried on all F-16 variants. They specify that only JP-4/JP-5 fuel is to be used in this tank.

70

Blue painted twenty-five pound practice bombs can be loaded on the Aerodynamic Triple Ejector Rack (TER). The Red Remove Before Flight tags are attached to the bomb safety wires.

The lower drag of the Aerodynamic Triple Ejector Rack (TER) is evident when viewed from head-on. This rack is loaded with Blue twenty-five pound practice bombs.

This Aerodynamic Triple Ejector Rack (TER) is preloaded with three Mk 82 low drag bombs (also known as Slicks). The Aerodynamic TER has far less drag than the earlier TER used on F-4s and F-105s.

This pylon is used to carry and launch the AIM-9 Sidewinder air-to-air missile. It is mounted at Stations 2 and 8 (outboard wing pylon) on all F-16 variants.

This F-16C is armed with AIM-9 Sidewinder missiles on the wing tip stations and AIM-120 AMRAAMs on the inboard wing stations. The F-16 can carry up to six AMRAAMs.

The groove in the Sidewinder launch pylon accepts the mounting lugs on the missile itself. This pylon can only be used to carry air-to-air missiles or a data link sensor pod for air combat maneuvering training.

This SUU-20 practice bomb dispenser is loaded on Station 3 (port inboard wing pylon). The SUU-20 carries small practice bombs and two rockets.

The ALQ-131 ECM pod is normally carried on the centerline of the F-16C. The ALQ-131 was one of the two ECM pods that saw widespread use during Operation DESERT STORM.

The Red Remove Before Flight flags are attached to the safety wires on the bomb fuzes loaded into this SUU-20 practice bomb dispenser. A flag is also attached to the dispenser jettison pin as well.

The ALQ-188 ECM pod on the centerline station is an older unit that is being replaced by the ALQ-131 and ALQ-119, although the ALQ-119 is also being phased out and is no longer widely used.

An AIM-9L Sidewinder air-to-air missile on the wing tip missile launch rail of an F-16C. The F-16C usually carries four AIM-9s for the air defense mission.

This F-16B is loaded with three AGM-65 Maverick TV-guided air-to-ground anti-tank missiles on a triple rack on the outboard wing pylon. The Sidewinder on the wing tip is an AIM-9L.

Missiles

Another Sidewinder variant that is carried by the F-16 is the AIM-9J Sidewinder. The latest variants of the Sidewinder have an all aspect capability.

This F-16C-42-CF is carrying the markings of the 9th AF commander and is armed with the newest air-to-air missile in the U.S. inventory, the AIM-120 AMRAMM. F-16Cs can carry six AIM-120s.

74

A TV guided Maverick air-to-ground missile loaded on a single missile rail carried on the outboard wing pylon on an F-16A. Normally, Mavericks are carried on triple launch rails.

The Maverick TV guided air-to-ground missile proved to be a valuable addition to the F-16's warload during Operation DESERT STORM. The TV guided missile can be used under all weather conditions.

This F-16C is carrying triple Maverick missile launch rails on the outboard wing pylon and an air-to-air missile pylon outboard of that. This F-16C is assigned to the 19th TFS Gamecocks at Shaw AFB, S.C. on 19 May 1986.

An armament crew uncrates and prepares a CBU-87 cluster bomb during Operation DESERT STORM. The CBU-87 was one of the most effective bombs carried by F-16s during the Gulf War.

Armorers carry an AIM-9L to its check stand during Operation DESERT STORM. Although it has been cleared to fire both the AIM-7 Sparrow and AIM-120 AMRAAM, until recently, the Sidewinder was the primary air-to-air missile for the F-16.

Armament crews crank 20MM cannon rounds into the ammunition drum of the M61 Vulcan cannon system on a 363rd Tactical Fighter Wing F-16C during Operation DESERT STORM.

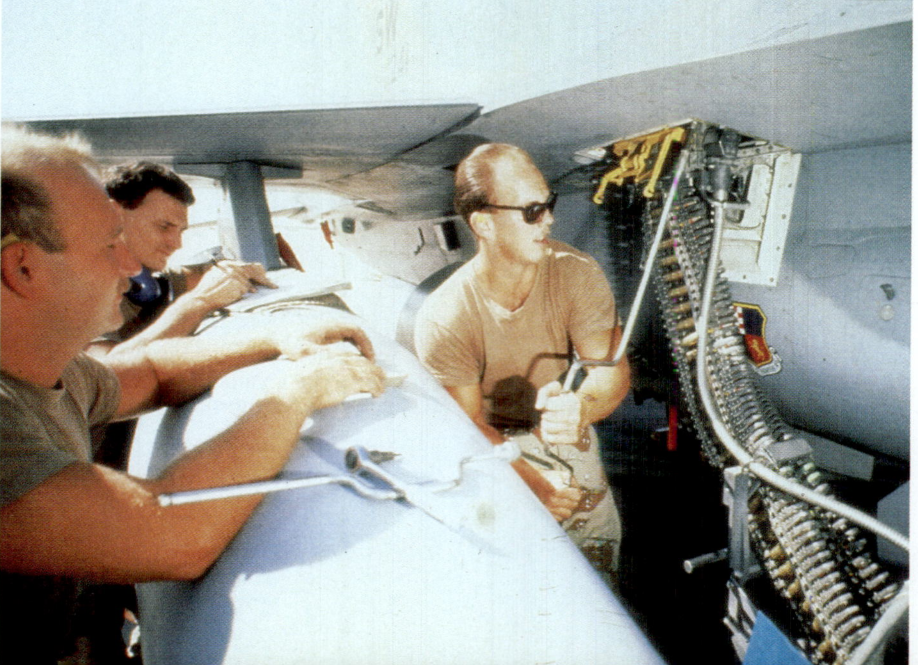

Among the differences on the F-16ADF variant is this four blade IFF antenna system installed in front of the windscreen. It is a bolt-on attachment not a production line change.

Besides the four antennas mounted in front of the canopy, the F-16ADF also carries a night identification searchlight on the port side of the nose

F-16 ADF

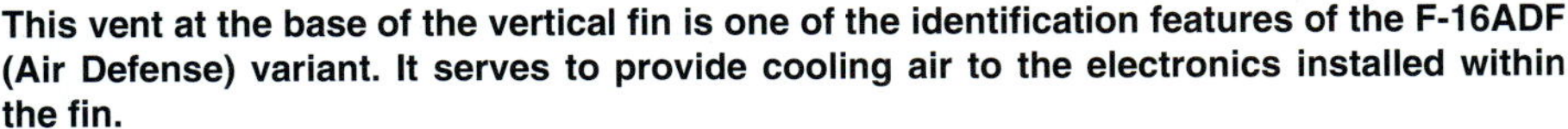

This vent at the base of the vertical fin is one of the identification features of the F-16ADF (Air Defense) variant. It serves to provide cooling air to the electronics installed within the fin.

This enlarged ECM antenna fairing is another identification feature of the F-16ADF. Most of these aircraft are modified F-16As and are primarily assigned to Air National Guard units.

An F-16C of the 17th TFS Hooters, 363rd TFW loaded with four AIM-9L Sidewinder missiles, an ALQ-119 ECM pod and three external fuel tanks during 1992.

This F-16 of the 5246th Test Squadron is loaded with a GBU-15 on the outboard wing station and a LGB on the inboard station.

Weapons crews load Mk 82 bombs on an old style Triple Ejector Rack of the type used on the F-4 Phantom. The F-16A was assigned to the 19th TFS at Shaw AFB, S.C. on 31 August 1983.

The ammunition drum and drive mechanism of the M61 gun system are undergoing servicing on this F-16B. The M61 Vulcan cannon system is installed on all variants of the Viper.

This F-16B has the skin panels over the M61 Vulcan 20MM six-barrel cannon ammunition drum and drive mechanism removed for maintenance.

Armament crews use an MJ-1 power bomb loader to load a CBU-59 Rockeye cluster bomb on the outboard wing pylon of an F-16C during Operation DESERT STORM.

A flight of F-16Cs of the 4thTFS head out for Iraqi targets during Operation DESERT STORM. They are armed with cluster bombs and four AIM-9 Sidewinder missiles.

A flight of F-16s from the Puerto Rican Air National Guard. The aircraft carry the unit insignia on the fuselage behind the cockpit.

An F-16ADF of the Texas Air National Guard taxies out for a mission armed with four AIM-9 Sidewinders and two 370 gallon wing tanks. These aircraft are based at Houston.

An F-16A of the Texas Air National Guard prepares to take on fuel from a KC-135 tanker. The refueling receptacle on the aircraft's spine is open and ready to receive the tanker's boom.